North Carolina Wildlife Animals & Mammals

Billy Grinslott – Kinsey Marie Books

ISBN - 9781968228439

Chipmunks are found in many areas. Chipmunks are small members of the squirrel family. They like to eat nuts and seeds. Chipmunks are most active during the day, especially at dawn and dusk. They have pouches inside of their cheeks so they can carry food. They are very friendly and will take food from your hand. Chipmunks need about 15 hours of sleep per day. The smallest chipmunk species is Tamias minimus, which is found throughout North America.

There are many squirrels in the wild. You may see a red or gray squirrel. The most popular is the gray squirrel. Squirrels are very acrobatic and can climb trees. Their favorite food is acorns. Squirrels hide their food in many small stashes and can find more than 90% of them later. Squirrels are fast and can run up a tree at 12 miles per hour. Newborn squirrels are blind, deaf, and hairless, and rely on their mother until they mature.

Flying Squirrels don't fly like birds. They don't have wings. They have skin that is attached to their legs. When they jump from a tree, they spread their legs out and glide through the air. Most glides are 30 feet from tree to tree. But they can glide up to 150 feet. They are primarily active at night and are social animals, often living in groups and sharing nests. They have large eyes for night vision, long whiskers for navigating in the dark, and a long, flattened tail for steering during glides.

Muskrats are found in marshes, ponds, and streams with abundant aquatic vegetation. Muskrats have a scaly tail that acts as a rudder for swimming and helps them stay afloat. They primarily eat aquatic plants like cattails, sedges, and grasses, but also consume small animals like mussels, crayfish, and fish. They have a second set of lips that close behind their front incisors, enabling them to dive underwater, chew, and eat without swallowing water. They build lodges made of mud and vegetation and also live in burrows along the banks of water sources.

There are many types of rabbits in the wild. The most common is the cottontail. Rabbits are cute, friendly, and fun to watch. Many people have rabbits for pets. They have soft fluffy fur. They are called cottontails because they have a white fluffy tail that looks like a cotton ball. Rabbits thrive in brushy areas, fields, and wooded habitats.

Marsh rabbits are smaller sized compared to other cottontail rabbits. Marsh rabbits are primarily active at night, spending their days resting in secluded areas. Marsh rabbits are exceptionally well-adapted to their wetland environment, spending a significant amount of time in the water. They are strong swimmers and often dive underwater to escape predators. Marsh rabbits have a smaller, more compact build than other cottontail rabbits. They have short ears, short legs, and a small, dark tail with a dark underside. Their hind legs have less fur and longer nails than cottontails, which helps them in swimming.

Pee-ewe what is that stinky critter with the big bushy tail. It smells bad. Skunks are normally curious and friendly unless you scare them. If you scare them, they will flip their bushy tale at you and spray you with a smelly potion and it stinks. Skunks spray a smelly, sulfur-based liquid from their anal glands as a defense mechanism. The spray can cause eye irritation and temporary blindness. Skunks are highly adaptable and can thrive in many different environments. Skunks have strong forefeet and long claws for digging. Skunks live in dens underground.

Spotted skunks are listed as a protected species. They are smaller than striped skunks and have a slenderer body. Unlike striped skunks, spotted skunks are excellent climbers and can scale trees and fences. When threatened, they stand on their front legs, turn their heads, and walk towards the predator, spraying their defensive spray. Before spraying, they also stamp their front feet on the ground to warn predators. They are primarily active at night and are known for being secretive.

Opossums or possums have strong tails and can hang from trees. One trick that a possum has, is when it feels danger is it will play dead. It will lay there and not move. Possums have white to gray face hair. Possums like to eat wood ticks. They are also immune to snakebites. Opossums are susceptible to frostbite because their hands and tails are not protected by fur. Opossums are marsupials, which means they have pouches for their young, like kangaroos and koalas.

Raccoons like to come out at night. Their eyes are made so they can see in the dark. Raccoons are highly intelligent and can solve problems. They can learn to open doors, trash cans, and other containers. They are called masked bandits because they like to raid and eat out of trash cans at night. Raccoons can survive in many environments.

Beavers use their teeth to cut and knock down trees. They build dams with them to block water, so they have a place to live and swim. They also eat wood. Beavers can stay underwater for about 8 minutes. Beavers slap their tails on the water to indicate danger. Beavers are the largest rodents in North America.

Nutria are large, semi-aquatic rodents known for their orange teeth and webbed hind feet. They are invasive in many areas, where they can cause significant damage. Their burrowing can destroy riverbanks and levees, and their diet of eating vegetation can decimate marshlands. Nutrias are larger than muskrats but smaller than beavers. Their large yellow-orange incisor teeth are used for gnawing and eating plants. Their partially webbed hind feet make them excellent swimmers. Nutrias have relatively poor eyesight and rely more on their hearing to detect danger. Unlike beavers and muskrats, they have a long, round, and mostly hairless tail.

Otters have the thickest fur of any animal. The otter is one of the few mammals that use tools, like rocks to break thing open. A group of otters resting together is called a raft.

Otters primarily rely on their sense of touch, whiskers, and forepaws, in murky waters to locate food. Otters have built in pouches of loose skin under their forearms to stash extra food when diving.

Groundhogs or woodchucks are the largest member of the squirrel family. Groundhogs get their name because of their big bodies, and they live underground. Groundhogs are skilled climbers and swimmers. Groundhogs are true hibernators, sleeping for up to six months. Groundhog Day is where Punxsutawney Phil predicts how long winter will last.

The American Mink lives across most of North America and is a cat sized. Mink are very skilled climbers and swimmers. They prefer to keep to themselves. They communicate using odors, visual signals, and other sounds. They purr when they're happy, like cats. Mink are agile swimmers, and they often dive to find food

Weasels are the smallest members of the meat-eating animals. Although small, they do not hibernate and are active all winter. Weasels in northern ranges turn white in the winter to camouflage in the snow. Weasels have long whiskers like cats, to help them feel things. They even have long whiskers on their elbows. When a weasel gets annoyed, it stomps its feet, just like humans do. Weasels are quick, agile, and alert animals. They are excellent climbers and swimmers.

Mallard ducks are by far the most recognizable and popular ducks in the world. They live in just about every area of North America. Their estimated population is around 19 million birds. The male is easily recognizable from its white neck ring and green neck and head. The female Mallard has between five to 14 light green eggs. Most ducks don't have green eggs, so this makes them unique. The male Mallard is called a drake and the female a hen. Female Mallards quack. Males don't quack, instead they produce deeper, raspier one- and two-note calls. They can also make rattling sounds by rubbing their bills against their flight feathers.

Canada Geese are the most sought after and abundant goose in North America. They live in many places. Canada geese can travel 1,500 miles in a day if the weather permits. Canada geese migrate every year. They fly in a V-formation, which allows them to travel long distances without stopping, as they can switch positions and conserve energy. Canada geese are known for their distinctive honk and are sometimes called Canadian honkers.

Yes, there are ruffed grouse in North Carolina, but they are primarily found in the mountainous regions, though populations have declined significantly due to habitat loss. Ruffed grouse are known for their drumming display, a sound produced by rapidly beating their wings. They use a series of thumps produced by their wings, creating a deep, resonating sound.

The American woodcock is a medium-sized bird that is typically found in wooded areas across North America. Woodcocks have large eyes, and their visual field is probably the largest of any bird, 360° in the horizontal plane, and 180° in the vertical plane. The American woodcock has earned a host of nick names including timberdoodle, night partridge, big-eye, bog sucker, and mud bat.

Mourning Doves are unable to sweat. To stay cool during hot weather, they pant just like dog do. Mourning doves eat and collect seeds in their crop, which is an enlarged part of their esophagus. Then they digest them later. It's estimated that there are more than 100 million mourning doves in the US. With the southern states having the biggest population.

The bobwhite quail has the largest range of any game bird in America. Bobwhite quail are the most common species of quail. The bobwhite is often referred to as the number one game bird of the eastern and southern United States. Bobwhite quail are known for their explosive flight, and social behavior in groups called coveys.

Wood ducks are by far one of the coolest looking birds. Males have vibrant colors and long feathers on the back of their head. Wood Ducks are unique among most waterfowl. They need bodies of water that are near trees. They use lakes, ponds, and streams that are adjacent to wooded areas so they can nest in tree cavities.

The Wild Turkey is a large, bird that is native to North America. It is the heaviest bird in the United States and can weigh up to 24 pounds. Only male turkey's gobble. Wild turkeys can fly. Wild turkeys sleep in trees. Their heads can change colors. You can tell a turkey's emotions by the color of their heads. Colors can change from red to blue to white, depending on how excited or calm they are. You can find wild turkeys in just about every state in America.

Bobcats are named for their short, bobbed tails with white tips. They have similar markings to lynxes but are much smaller. Bobcats live in a variety of habitats. Bobcats are skilled at leaping and can run up to 30 miles per hour.

Gray fox prefers to live in rocky canyons and ridges but can also be found in wooded areas and open fields. They have strong, hooked claws that enable them to climb trees. Which is abnormal for a dog species. Gray foxes are not observed as frequently as red foxes due to their reclusive nature and more nocturnal habits.

Red foxes have excellent hearing, allowing them to hear rodents digging underground from miles away. When afraid, red foxes grin or look like they are smiling. Red fox's front paws have five toes, while their hind feet only have four. Foxes dig underground dens where they raise their kits and hide from predators. A group of foxes is called a skulk or a leash. Babys are called kits and females are called vixens.

The coyote is bigger than a fox weighing between 20 and 45 pounds. Eastern coyotes are part wolf. Coyotes are great for pest control. They like to eat mice and rats. They can adapt and live almost anywhere, even in the city. Coyotes are very smart and have been observed learning and following traffic signals in some cities. They have a yip type of call when they communicate with each other. Coyotes are found in all the United States, except Hawaii.

The Coywolf got its name because it is a cross between the Coyote and the Wolf. While coyotes are common, they are smaller than wolves. Coyotes typically weigh around 30-40 pounds, while coywolf hybrids can weigh significantly more, with some reports suggesting specimens of over 60 pounds. They can be significantly larger than a typical coyote.

Red wolves are smaller than gray wolves but larger than coyotes. They are known for their reddish colored fur. The critically endangered Red Wolf exists in the wild only in the coastal plains of extreme northeastern North Carolina, primarily around the Alligator River National Wildlife Refuge. Red wolves are known for being the world's most endangered wolf, there's only a couple dozen left in the U.S.

Yes, there are feral hogs, often called wild boars or hogs, in North Carolina. They are an invasive species found in numerous counties. Feral hogs are also known as wild boars or wild pigs. Feral hogs are known for their high reproductive rates and their tendency to root up the ground, which can lead to habitat destruction. They are highly intelligent, social animals with a keen sense of smell and a surprisingly good memory. Wild pigs can be found in various habitats, including forests, grasslands, and agricultural areas.

Armadillos are known for their unique armor-like shells. Armadillos are the only living mammals with a hard shell, made of true bone and consisting of bands of plates connected by flexible skin. When threatened they can roll up into a ball and their shell protects them. Armadillos are primarily nocturnal animals, spending their days in burrows and emerging at night to forage for food. They are excellent diggers, using their strong claws and legs to burrow into the ground and forage for food, which primarily consists of insects and grubs. They also like to eat ant and termites.

Black bears are the smallest members of the bear family in North America. Black Bears love to eat sweet things like berries, fruits, and vegetables. They are good climbers and fast runners. They are excellent swimmers and can paddle at least a mile and a half in freshwater. They usually sleep for long periods of time and hibernate during the winter. They typically try to stay away from people unless they find food in the area.

The whitetail deer is the most popular deer in North America. Whitetail deer have good eyesight and hearing. They can detect small sounds from a quarter of a mile away. Only male deer grow antlers, which are shed each year. Whitetail deer are good swimmers and will use large streams and lakes to escape predators. A young deer is called a fawn, a male is a buck, and a female is called a doe. They are the most common deer species and live everywhere in North America.

Elk are the second largest members of the deer family. Bulls can weigh up to 1,100 lbs. Elk antlers can grow up to an inch per day. They can run 40 miles per hour and outrun horses. Elk have a good sense of hearing and can swivel their ears back and forth. Elk have eyes on the sides of their heads and can see in every direction except directly in front or behind. They make a cool bugling sound when communicating with other elk. It's fun to listen to them.

North Carolina has wild horses, specifically Colonial Spanish Mustangs, known as Banker horses, living on the Outer Banks barrier islands, with large herds in Corolla and Shackleford Banks. These feral horses are descendants of animals brought by Spanish explorers centuries ago and are protected as the state horse, roaming freely on the dunes and beaches.

Alligators can't digest salt, so they live in freshwater environments like ponds, marshes, wetlands, and swamps. Male alligators can grow up to 15 feet long. Alligators Walk with their legs directly beneath them, which allows them to lift their tails off the ground. Alligators are the loudest reptiles in the world, with roars that can reach up to 90 decibels. Alligators eat a variety of foods, including bugs, amphibians, small fish, fruit, snakes, turtles, birds, and mammals. Alligators can regrow lost teeth, they have up to 80 in their mouth at one time. They can lose over 2,000 teeth in their lifetime and regrow them. They can see in the dark and their eyes glow when a light is shined on them.

Fun Facts about North Carolina Animals

1 - The Eastern Gray Squirrel is North Carolina's official state mammal.

2 - The Virginia Opossum is North Carolina's only marsupial that can eat venomous snakes.

3 - NC is a key area for the reintroduced red wolf, a rare canid.

4 - North Carolina boasts the largest black bear population in the Southeast.

5 – Bobcats are the only wild cat in NC; they can adapt to many habitats.

6 - Flying Squirrels are nocturnal squirrels that glide through the air and are rarely seen by humans.

7 - Wild Boars, called feral hogs, are also present.

8 – The American Alligator is the state's largest reptile.

9 – Elk have been reintroduced and thrive in the Great Smoky Mountains.

10 – Raccoons are famous for raiding garbage cans at night.

Author Page

Billy Grinslott - Kinsey Marie Books

ISBN – 9781968228439

Thanks

www.ingramcontent.com/pod-product-compliance
Lightning Source LLC
Chambersburg PA
CBHW060852270326
41934CB00002B/100